*gorgeous garlic*

Rio Nuevo Publishers®
P.O. Box 5250, Tucson, Arizona 85703-0250
(520) 623-9558, www.rionuevo.com

Text and illustrations © 2006 by Rio Nuevo Publishers. Food
styling by Tracy Vega. Many thanks to AJ's Fine Foods and to
Jeannine Brookshire for providing beautiful settings and amenities
for the photo shoots for this book.

Photography credits as follows:
W. Ross Humphreys: pages 2-3, 4 (left), 16, 30, 37, back cover
Robin Stancliff: pages 4 (right), 5, 12, 21, 25, 45, 55, 56, 65, front cover

Library of Congress Cataloging-in-Publication Data
Grimes, Gwin Grogan.
Gorgeous garlic / Gwin Grogan Grimes.
    p. cm.—— (Cook west series)
Includes index.
ISBN-13: 978-1-887896-93-1 (pbk.)
ISBN-10: 1-887896-93-7 (pbk.)
1. Cookery (Garlic) 2. Cookery, American—Southwestern
style. I. Title. II. Series.
TX819.G3G75 2006
641.6'526—dc22

                          2006000387

Design: Karen Schober, Seattle, Washington.
Printed in Korea.
10  9  8  7  6  5  4  3  2  1

# gorgeous
## *garlic*

GWIN GROGAN GRIMES

RIO NUEVO PUBLISHERS
TUCSON, ARIZONA

COOK WEST
SERIES

# contents

xxxxxx

"I can't cook without garlic!"

I've heard so many people say this, from celebrity chefs on television to cookbook authors, cooking teachers, and home cooks, that it must be true. It certainly is for me.

A passion for garlic has existed the world over for centuries. Among the historic figures reputed to be garlic fans: Hippocrates, Pliny, Aristophanes, Homer, and Nero. The poet Lord Byron subsisted on an idiosyncratic list of foods that included garlic stew. Garlic is even mentioned in the Bible, as one of the six items of food that the Hebrews missed from their time in Egypt.

Garlic is thought to have been among the second wave of food crops brought to the Caribbean by the Europeans who first explored the New World. It was certainly among the first foods carried into New Mexico, Arizona, and Texas by Spanish missionaries and colonists, and was commonly grown in kitchen gardens for both churches and families alike. Today, California is the U.S. leader in garlic production, and the town of Gilroy, California—the self-proclaimed "Garlic Capital of the World"—hosts its annual Garlic Festival every July.

Garlic consumption in this country has soared since the 1990s and continues to rise, according to the U.S. Department of Agriculture. Americans eat more than 3 pounds per person per year. Once considered an ethnic ingredient and far too pungent for "elegant" cuisine, garlic is not only mainstream today, it's almost ubiquitous. A quick stroll through any supermarket will yield roasted garlic salad dressing, fancy garlic mustard, garlic-spiked sea salt—even the venerable Tabasco brand now has a garlic-laced pepper sauce. To this, I say "Hooray!"

I'll take garlic almost any way I can get it—except maybe dessert. I know about the recipes out there for garlic ice cream and garlic crème brûlée, but I'll leave that to others. I'll stick with everything savory flavored, stuffed, or rubbed with garlic.

One of my first, and fondest, memories of cooking involves garlic. My father was the typical mid-century male barbecue wrangler, but with a twist. His specialty involved the gas grill, a fancy electric rotisserie, and what seemed to me like an entire side of beef. I know now that the beef was actually no more than a large sirloin tip, usually cut just for him by the butcher after a serious discussion weighing the merits of various slabs of Angus. I don't think he ever picked one out of the case.

Back home, it was my job to cram whole cloves of garlic into the slits my father riddled the beef with, using his thin-bladed boning knife. I had short, skinny fingers perfect for the job. Even then, I didn't mind that my hands reeked of garlic for a couple of days afterward.

Now when I think back on it, it seems that maybe I should have been grossed out by handling raw meat. Not me. I knew that a few hours later I'd be eating roast beef better than any found in a restaurant, and I loved what became a ritual for my father and me.

But that's not my only recollection of garlic. I've got fond memories of garlic bread at a favorite Italian restaurant, garlicky tzatziki sauce on a festival gyro, my first bite of roasted garlic mashed potatoes... I'm getting hungry just thinking about it.

I hope you'll find the meals you make with these recipes to be memorable, too.

**MAKING THE MOST OF IT**    *Selection and storage* Heads of garlic should be full and firm, with cloves ranging from pure white to tan to dark purple and every shade in between. If it feels dried up, discard.

Starting to sprout? Toss, or plant in your garden. If I suspect a clove is past its prime, I always slice it in half lengthwise, then pry out the green shoot in the center and throw it away because it will be bitter. Store garlic in a well-ventilated, cool place, but not in a plastic bag. Don't store fresh garlic in the refrigerator, as it will mold. Garlic jars with holes in them are cute, but not required. Don't separate or peel cloves until you're ready to use them. Once roasted or toasted, garlic *should* be stored in the refrigerator. Ditto for garlic oil, which has a nasty propensity toward botulism at room temperature. Keep it cold, keep it safe! Dried garlic is clearly inferior to fresh; however, if you must use it, look for granulated garlic, not garlic powder or garlic salt. I've used dried garlic in one recipe here, a dry barbecue rub.

*Equipment* The recipes in this book were created and tested in a standard home kitchen—mine—with ordinary equipment. Except maybe for the dozen or so garlic presses, choppers, slicers, and other gadgets that I bought to test for this book, I used only the basics. I have tried every single garlic press I could find on the market, from dollar-store cheapies (all plastic) to a mind-boggling Garlic Genius that certainly outwitted me (it's still in pieces on my kitchen counter). Many serviceable presses are available in the $10–$20 range. Look for features such as a comfortable grip, large hopper, and ease of cleaning. That's it.

*Measuring garlic* All the recipes in this book measure garlic in cloves instead of teaspoons or tablespoons, for simplicity's sake. Who wants to chop a clove, measure, chop a little more, measure, and then end up with a little too much or not enough? Chances are, I'm just going to toss it all in, anyway. If your cloves seem small, use two instead of one. Because every head of garlic is going to vary, the key is to season, cook, and taste, adjusting as you go along. You may like a little more or a little less.

*Peeling, mincing, pureeing, etc.* From whole clove to puree, garlic can be halved, sliced, chopped, minced, crushed or pressed, or pureed in a blender or food processor. For the smoothest possible paste, you'll need to add a bit of liquid. Garlic can be pureed using a chef's knife: mince the garlic, sprinkling with a bit of salt. Then begin mashing the mixture with the side of the knife, chopping and mashing until pureed. The easiest way to peel whole cloves of garlic is to lay them individually on the cutting board, then press with the heel of your hand. You can also use a wide knife blade. Place a garlic clove on the cutting board and, with the flat side of the knife blade down and the blade facing away from you, press down slowly but firmly with your fist. The easiest way to separate cloves from a head of garlic is to turn the head upside down (root side up) on a cutting board and press down firmly. The pressure will separate the cloves.

*Cooking tips* When you sauté vegetables such as onion, peppers, and garlic, make sure to add the garlic last, near the end of the cooking. It usually is chopped finer and, because it contains proportionately less water than the other vegetables, it will burn much faster. Burned garlic is bitter garlic! One way to avoid burning garlic in a sauté is to leave it whole, then mash it after it's been cooking a while. Some chefs believe that the finer you cut garlic, the more bitter it becomes because more of the cell walls are crushed as it is processed. My goal is to simply disperse the garlic as evenly as possible throughout the recipe, making sure that the resulting dish has a pleasant texture.

*Garlic odors*  The best way to remove garlic odor from your hands is with soap, water, and a nail brush. As far as removing garlic from your breath, try chewing on a little parsley or swallowing some parsley oil caplets (sold commercially as breath freshener pills) after a garlic-laden meal.

**TO YOUR HEALTH!**

Historically, garlic has been used to treat all manner of illness from acne to smallpox, and just about everything in between. It was revered among ancient Egyptians and Chinese for its medicinal properties. Garlic is one of the oldest cultivated foods in the world, and its use for medical and religious purposes—and eating, of course—has been documented for more than 4,000 years. Its three primary health benefits are said to be cardiovascular, antimicrobial, and reduction or inhibition of tumors. Also, it is thought to reduce cholesterol, prevent blood clots and strokes, and reduce blood pressure. These properties are attributed to allicin, a sulphur compound found in the bulb. Scientific studies are being conducted all the time to learn more of its medicinal uses. The American Dietetic Association's report on functional foods—that is, things we eat that also can promote health—concludes that scientific research shows that one fresh garlic clove per day is enough to help reduce blood pressure and serum cholesterol.

## Roasted Garlic

XXXXXX

*This is it—the foundation for so many great recipes. Roasting garlic mellows any bitter flavor it might have and brings out its natural sweetness. It's also delicious squeezed out of the papery skin directly onto French bread. Instant garlic bread!*

*Makes about ½ cup*

**4 whole heads of garlic, preferably with big, firm cloves**

**2 tablespoons olive oil**

Preheat oven to 350 degrees F.

Line a baking dish with aluminum foil or parchment paper, then follow one of these two methods:

If you want to end up with whole cloves, stand the garlic heads upright (root side down) in the baking dish, drizzle them with olive oil, and bake them until tender, about 25–40 minutes, depending on the size of the cloves. Let them cool until the garlic can be handled, then separate the cloves and remove their papery skins. (This method tends to get a little messy.)

For mashed garlic, trim the top quarter of each garlic head, exposing the tops of the cloves. Drizzle with oil and bake as directed above. When the garlic heads cool enough to handle, simply squeeze out the garlic from the papery skin.

Roasted garlic can be made ahead and stored in the refrigerator for up to a week.

## Toasted Garlic and Garlic Oil

xxxxx

*Makes ½ cup of oil and about 2 tablespoons toasted garlic*

¼ **cup olive oil**

**6 large cloves garlic, minced or whole, depending on how you want to use it**

*Toasted garlic has the same mellow depth of flavor as garlic roasted in the oven, but with a crisp exterior. It's great in many different recipes, but really shines when served in its cooking oil with a big hunk of French bread.*

In a small saucepan over medium heat, combine the olive oil and garlic. Simmer for about 5 minutes, watching closely, as the garlic will brown quickly.

The garlic is done when it's golden to medium brown and crisp. If it's too dark it will be bitter.

Strain the oil to separate it from the garlic, reserving both. Store the oil in the refrigerator. It may become thick and cloudy but will return to normal at room temperature. You can store toasted garlic in a small dish or plastic bag in the refrigerator. The oil and the toasted garlic will keep for at least a week refrigerated.

## Garlic Butter

xxxxx

*Compound butters are a cook's secret weapon. They can be flavored with an endless combination of spices, herbs, and other seasonings, then stored in the freezer or refrigerator until needed. Use them as a condiment on meat, vegetables, rice, and other grains, or as pasta sauce. Cook with them or serve them at the table to spread on hot French bread. Put a log or pretty molded butter on a plate, surround it with fancy crackers, and call it an appetizer. Compound butter is your friend!*

Mash the butter, garlic, and parsley together in a small bowl. Form into a round log and wrap in wax or parchment paper. Refrigerate to firm, or use immediately. For longer storage, place the paper-wrapped log in a plastic bag and freeze it. Slice off as much as you need and return the remainder to the freezer.

Alternately, you can mix the butter and garlic, then roll the log in the chopped parsley. This makes very pretty green-crusted circles when you dot a steak hot off the grill or a boneless, skinless chicken breast right from the broiler.

This is the most basic version. Feel free to create your own combinations with your favorite herbs and spices. Some suggestions to get you going: garlic, lemon zest, and fresh thyme for chicken or fish; garlic, Tabasco sauce, and coarse-ground black pepper for steak; garlic, ground cumin, and lime zest for new potatoes; toasted garlic, oregano, and minced sun-dried tomatoes for pasta. The only caveat is to avoid too much liquid seasoning, such as Worcestershire or citrus juice—a little bit is fine, but too much will prevent a good emulsion. Instead, think about using citrus zest or pure citrus oils. Also, you'll find Worcestershire powder among the various dried spices at your supermarket.

*Makes ½ cup*

1 stick (8 tablespoons) unsalted butter, softened

4 cloves roasted garlic (see page 13) or 2 cloves raw garlic, minced or pressed, or a combination

1 tablespoon minced fresh parsley

# Garlic and Lime Salsa

xxxxxx

*This is a variation of my friend Paula's classic salsa recipe. We like to say it's not a party until she shows up with her salsa and a bag of tortilla chips. Because it's difficult to predict how hot your jalapeños are going to be or how sweet your onions, the key is to taste, taste, taste until you get it just right.*

Place the tomatoes, onion, jalapeño, and garlic in a food processor fitted with a metal blade. Pulse a few times until the desired texture is reached. Pour the mixture into a non-reactive bowl and stir in the lime juice, cilantro, and a pinch of salt. Cover and refrigerate for several hours to allow the flavors to blend and mellow.

Taste and adjust the seasonings as needed before serving.

This recipe can be scaled up as needed, but watch the jalapeño!

*Serves 4*

5 Roma tomatoes, peeled, seeded, and roughly chopped, or 1 can (15 ounces) diced tomatoes

1 small onion, trimmed, peeled, and diced

1 large jalapeño, stem removed and roughly chopped (seeded if desired)

3 cloves garlic, roughly chopped

Juice of 1 lime

$1/4$ cup cilantro leaves

Salt

## Black Bean–Toasted Garlic Pico de Gallo

xxxxxx

*Serves 8*

1 can (15 ounces) black beans, rinsed and drained

1 can (11 ounces) extra-sweet corn, rinsed and drained

1/4 cup finely chopped red bell pepper

1/4 cup finely chopped purple onion

1–2 jalapeños, stems removed, seeded, and finely chopped

1 tablespoon toasted minced garlic (see recipe on page 14)

1/4 cup chopped cilantro leaves

1 clove garlic, pressed or minced

Juice of 1 lime

*The key to producing a picture-perfect pico is to make sure all the vegetables are about the same size. Don't be alarmed by the cans of black beans and corn—their texture works well in this recipe. While you may substitute your own homemade black beans and fresh corn cut right off the cob, don't try frozen corn—it will make the pico mushy.*

Mix all the ingredients in a medium-size bowl. Cover with plastic wrap and chill for several hours to meld the flavors.

Serve with tortilla chips or with grilled meats or fish.

## Double Garlic Dip

xxxxxx

*Serves 4*

1 cup sour cream

5 cloves roasted garlic, mashed

2 cloves raw garlic, pressed

1/4 teaspoon lemon-pepper seasoning

1/4 cup grated Parmigiano-Reggiano cheese

*Don't be misled by how few ingredients are listed for this recipe. This full-flavored dip takes advantage of both the piquancy of raw garlic and the sweet depth of roasted garlic. The key is to refrigerate it for a while to meld the flavors before serving, even overnight. This recipe can be easily doubled or tripled.*

Mix all the ingredients in a small bowl. Cover and chill for at least 2 hours to meld the flavors. Taste and adjust the seasonings before serving.

Serve with potato chips or vegetables for dipping.

## Garlic Chile con Queso

xxxxxx

*This* queso *is right at home when served with crisp tortilla chips or as the sauce for a pan of enchiladas. Try a variety of cheeses to come up with the combination you like best. Just avoid the processed orange stuff!*

Heat a saucepan over medium to medium-high heat and add the oil. When the oil shimmers, add onion and garlic and sauté until they are softened and clear.

Add jalapeños and tomatoes. Turn the heat down to low and add grated Cheddar and Monterey Jack cheeses, stirring until melted. Add sour cream and stir well. Do not allow the mixture to boil. When it is warmed through, remove from heat and serve.

*Serving tip:* Keep warm in a slow cooker set on low heat.

*Serves 6–8*

1 tablespoon olive or vegetable oil

1 cup finely chopped white or yellow onion

6 cloves garlic, minced or put through a garlic press

1–2 fresh jalapeños, seeds and stems removed, finely chopped

1 can (14–15 ounces) chopped tomatoes, drained

8 ounces Cheddar cheese, grated

8 ounces Monterey Jack cheese, grated

1 cup sour cream

## Garlic Spinach Crab Dip

xxxxxx

*Serves 6–8*

Cooking spray

1 package frozen spinach, thawed

1 cup mayonnaise

1/2 cup grated Parmigiano-Reggiano cheese

1/2 cup grated *queso quesadilla* or Oaxaca cheese (or substitute Monterey Jack)

6 cloves garlic, minced

1 1/2 pounds fresh crabmeat, picked over to remove any bits of shell

*Choose a pretty ovenproof dish so you can bake and serve with less mess, or divide the dip into individual ramekins and serve with slices of French bread for an elegant starter at a sit-down dinner. This recipe can be doubled or tripled as necessary.*

Preheat the oven to 350 degrees F.

Coat an 8 x 8-inch casserole dish with cooking spray.

Press the excess moisture from the thawed spinach. In a medium-size bowl, mix the mayonnaise, Parmigiano-Reggiano, *queso quesadilla* (or substitute), garlic, and spinach until blended. Gently fold in the crabmeat and scrape the dip into the prepared casserole dish.

Bake for about 15 minutes, or until the mixture is hot and bubbly. Serve with baguette slices or tortilla chips.

## Garlic-Soy Chicken Wings

xxxxxx

*Serves 8*

½ cup soy sauce

3 cloves garlic, minced

¼ cup sugar

½ cup dark brown sugar

3 dozen chicken drummettes or 18 chicken wings

*These little tidbits pack lots of flavor, which is probably why they were one of my most popular appetizers when I was a caterer. I loved them because they required so few ingredients, they kept well in a chafing dish, and they reheated beautifully.*

Preheat the oven to 350 degrees F.

In a small bowl, mix the soy sauce, garlic, sugar, and dark brown sugar. Place the chicken in a large roasting pan, nestling the pieces close together so they will all fit in one pan. Pour the soy mixture over the chicken and place the pan in the oven. Bake for about 30 minutes, then remove from the oven and turn over the chicken. Return to the oven and bake another 30 minutes. Remove, turn over again, and bake for a final 20 minutes. The chicken pieces will be dark brown, and the meat falling-off-the-bone tender.

## Brie Baked with Roasted Garlic and Chiles

xxxxxx

*This is a version of an appetizer I taught in a class featuring Hatch green chiles, which Texans just go crazy for. I had no idea that this dish—a variation on a classic—would turn out to be so popular. Don't be afraid to work with phyllo; in this recipe, the wrapping doesn't need to be perfect. Patch all you want, brush it with butter, and it will turn out fine.*

Unwrap the cheese and place the round on a plate. Pierce the top of it with the tip of a knife in several places, then drizzle the Cognac or brandy over the cheese. Let this stand at room temperature while you prepare the other ingredients.

Squeeze the garlic cloves out of their skins and mash them together with the olive oil in a small bowl to form a paste. Spread roasted garlic paste on top of the Brie. Arrange chiles on top of the garlic paste, followed by piñon nuts. Set this aside.

Lay the phyllo dough sheets on a dry work surface and cover them with a damp towel. On a baking sheet lined with parchment paper or a Silpat nonstick mat, place one square of phyllo. Brush it lightly with some of the melted butter. Repeat the process with 4 more sheets, overlapping slightly as you stack them. Place 1 layer of phyllo on top of the cheese round and brush it lightly with butter. Repeat the process with 4 more sheets, laying each one at an angle to the previous one. Pick up the cheese round and tuck the overhanging edges of phyllo under it, then center the cheese on the sheets of dough on the baking sheet. Gather up the edges of the bottom layers of phyllo, and gather them loosely on top of the cheese. Brush with butter. Take any leftover pieces of phyllo that may have broken off and gather them at the top of the cheese, brushing the outside with butter. Cover the Brie loosely with plastic wrap and refrigerate until ready to bake.

About 30 minutes before serving, preheat the oven to 400 degrees F. Place the prepared Brie in the oven and bake for 20 minutes, or until lightly browned. Remove from the oven and let cool for 10 minutes.

*Serves 8*

1 mini Brie (1 pound)

1 tablespoon Cognac or brandy

1 head roasted garlic (see page 13)

1–2 teaspoons extra-virgin olive oil

1/4 cup roasted mild Hatch chiles

1/4 cup piñon nuts, toasted

10 sheets phyllo dough, thawed and cut into 12-inch squares

8 tablespoons (1 stick) unsalted butter, melted

## Shrimp Mojo de Ajo

XXXXXX

*Serves 4*

2 tablespoons unsalted butter, divided

1 pound shrimp (21–25 per pound), rinsed, shelled, and deveined

6 cloves garlic, minced

Juice of 1 lemon

1/4 teaspoon oregano

1/2 teaspoon garlic-flavored Tabasco

1 tablespoon finely chopped cilantro leaves

Pinch of salt

Pinch of freshly ground black pepper

*Literally translated from the Spanish,* mojo de ajo *means "gravy of garlic." I just think of it as "delicious," and order it every time I see it on a menu. I've tried the bottled mojo marinade, but it's salty and has too many artificial ingredients for my taste. It's easier—and cheaper—to make it from scratch.*

Preheat the oven to 450 degrees F.

Prepare a shallow pan or ovenproof baking dish by greasing it with some of the unsalted butter. Lay shrimp in one layer on the bottom of the baking dish.

In a small bowl, mix the garlic, lemon juice, oregano, Tabasco, cilantro, salt, and pepper. Pour this mixture over the shrimp in the dish. Dot with the remaining butter.

Place the baking dish in the oven and cook for about 5 minutes, or until the shrimp turn pink and opaque.

Serve immediately with French bread for sopping up the leftover juices.

## Garlic Cheese-Stuffed Jalapeño Peppers

xxxxxx

*Serves 6*

12 large fresh jalapeños

6 cloves garlic, minced

1/3 cup minced purple onion

1/4 cup minced red bell pepper

1/4 cup cream cheese

1/4 cup shredded *queso quesadilla* or Oaxaca cheese (or substitute Monterey Jack)

1/2 pound thick-sliced bacon, each piece cut in half

1/2 cup *crema* (Mexican-style sour cream)

*It's surprising how many people who say they don't eat jalapeños will scarf down a few of these tasty bites. Perfect for an appetizer served with a frosty margarita or ice-cold cerveza. In the summer, try cooking these on the grill.*

Line a sheet pan with aluminum foil or parchment paper.

Slice off the stem ends of the jalapeños and scoop out the seeds, creating hollows for the stuffing.

Mix the garlic, onion, bell pepper, and cheeses in a small bowl. Stuff each jalapeño with the cheese mixture and wrap it with a piece of bacon, securing with 2 toothpicks.

Turn on the broiler in the oven. Broil the bacon-wrapped peppers for about 10–15 minutes, then remove them from the oven and turn each one over. Return to the broiler for another 8 minutes or so, until the bacon is browned.

Serve immediately, drizzled with a bit of *crema*.

## Pistachio Pesto Pinwheels

XXXXXX

*Pistachios are a nontraditional substitute for piñon nuts in this basil pesto recipe. Both kinds of nuts are grown in the southwestern United States, so pick your favorite. Other substitutions can include replacing some of the basil with cilantro or flat-leaf parsley and switching the Parmesan with Asiago or Manchego cheese. Note that you will need to thaw the frozen puff pastry overnight before starting to prepare this dish.*

Remove the package of puff pastry from the refrigerator.

Put the basil, pistachios, and garlic in a food processor fitted with a metal blade. Pulse several times until all the ingredients are chopped finely and evenly. With the blade running, drizzle in a stream of olive oil until a smooth paste is formed. Add the cheese, pulsing a few times until the mixture is blended into pesto. It will be a bit thicker than the pesto used to sauce pasta. If needed, add more olive oil, a little at a time, until the pesto is easy to spread.

Unwrap and unfold the puff pastry sheets, flattening the fold "seams" with your fingers. With a pastry brush, spread a thin, even layer of pesto over each sheet, leaving about a ¼-inch border on one narrow end.

One at a time, roll up each sheet like a jellyroll. When you get to the end, dampen the end edge with a bit of water and seal the roll closed. Handling the pastry softens it, so to make it easier to slice into even rounds, wrap each roll in plastic wrap

*Serves 8–10*

**1 package frozen puff pastry (2 sheets), thawed overnight in refrigerator**

**1 cup basil leaves, stems removed**

**3 tablespoons shelled pistachios**

**4 cloves garlic, trimmed**

**¼–½ cup extra-virgin olive oil**

**½ cup shredded Parmigiano-Reggiano cheese**

**Cooking spray (optional)**

or wax paper and refrigerate. For longer storage, insert the wrapped rolls into freezer storage bags and freeze them.

Preheat the oven to 425 degrees F.

Prepare your baking sheets by coating them with baking spray or lining them with parchment paper.

After about an hour, or as long as it takes the pastry to firm up, slice into ¼-inch slices and lay the slices on the baking sheets so the spiral of pastry and pesto faces up.

Bake for about 15–20 minutes, or until the pastry is puffed and lightly golden brown. Serve warm for best results.

If baking earlier in the day, do not refrigerate the baked pastries or they will get soggy. Cover with a clean dish towel, then pop them into a warm oven and re-heat for a few minutes before serving.

## Roasted Garlic Quesadillas

xxxxxx

*Essentially a grilled cheese sandwich with a Mexican accent, the quesadilla is the perfect marriage of cheese (queso) and flatbread (tortilla). Experiment with your favorite ingredients to create your own tasty combinations.*

Sauté the onion with a little oil until translucent; add mushrooms and continue to cook until just tender.

Mix the onion/mushroom mixture with the chiles, garlic, and cheese in a medium-size bowl.

Heat a skillet over medium heat and coat it with cooking spray. Cover the skillet with as many tortillas as you can fit at one time, and spoon some of the vegetable-cheese mixture over each one. Sprinkle with bacon, if desired. Top with another tortilla. Cook until the bottom tortillas began to turn golden and the cheese starts to melt. Carefully turn over each quesadilla and cook a little longer, until the other side is also crisp and golden. Slide each quesdilla onto a cutting board and cut it into wedges. Serve while hot.

*Serves 6 as a first course*

1 small onion, diced

1 tablespoon olive or vegetable oil

1/2 pound mushrooms, sliced

2 roasted green chiles, julienned

1 head roasted garlic, removed from skins and mashed (see page 13)

1/2 pound mild white cheese, such as Oaxaca or Monterey Jack, grated

Cooking spray

12 flour tortillas, about 8 inches each

6 strips bacon, chopped and cooked until crisp (optional)

## Garlic Balsamic Vinaigrette

xxxxxx

*Why buy commercial salad dressing when it's so easy to make at home? This recipe is made from pantry staples, and you can make as much or as little as you need at the time. Dijon mustard flavors the vinaigrette, but more importantly it acts as an emulsifier to help keep the oil and the vinegar suspended in a solution instead of separating. It's more than a visual effect—your dressing will taste better!*

In a small bowl, combine the vinegar, mustard, and honey. While whisking with one hand, slowly and evenly pour in the olive oil with the other hand to form a smooth emulsion. Stir in the garlic and season with salt and pepper to taste.

*Serves 4*

$1/4$ **cup balsamic vinegar**

**1 tablespoon Dijon mustard**

**1 teaspoon honey**

$3/4$ **cup extra-virgin olive oil**

**2 cloves garlic, pressed or minced**

**Kosher salt**

**Freshly ground black pepper**

## Creamy Garlic Ranch Dressing

xxxxxx

*Serves 6*

3/4 **cup sour cream**

1/2 **cup mayonnaise**

1/4 **cup buttermilk**

1/4 **cup chopped fresh flat-leaf parsley**

1/4 **cup chopped fresh chives**

4 **cloves garlic, minced**

1/4 **teaspoon kosher salt, or to taste**

1/2 **teaspoon freshly ground black pepper, or to taste**

*It's a classic, but amped up with lots of raw garlic and fresh herbs. This dressing works equally as well as a dip for vegetables or chips. For a spicier concoction, add a little cayenne pepper or a few shakes of Tabasco.*

Whisk together the sour cream, mayonnaise, buttermilk, parsley, chives, garlic, salt, and pepper in a bowl until well combined.

Chill, covered, until slightly thickened, at least 1 hour (for the flavors to develop). Taste and adjust the seasoning. If it seems too thick to pour, add a little more buttermilk.

This dressing can be made a few days ahead and stored, covered, in the refrigerator.

# Garlic, Jicama, and Pineapple Salad

xxxxxx

*This sweet and slightly piquant salad would also work well as a salsa to serve with grilled chicken or fish. Or just add chips and you've got an appetizer.*

Whisk together the oil, vinegar, garlic, cilantro, and cumin in a small bowl to blend. Season with salt and pepper to taste.

Combine jicama and pineapple in a bowl and toss with just enough dressing to coat evenly.

*Serves 4*

$1/_3$ cup canola oil

3 tablespoons white wine vinegar or sherry vinegar

1 tablespoon minced garlic

$1/_4$ cup chopped fresh cilantro leaves

$1/_4$ teaspoon ground cumin

Salt

Freshly ground black pepper

1 small jicama, grated with largest holes of grater

1 cup diced fresh pineapple

## Cool-as-a-Cucumber Salad

xxxxxx

*While this seems to me to be a quintessentially summer dish, I sometimes crave it at other times of the year. English cucumbers, generally seedless, can be found in the produce department of most supermarkets year-round. Look for the skinny, slightly creased cucumbers, almost always wrapped individually in plastic.*

Measure out the vinegar in a small liquid measuring cup. Add garlic and a few grindings of black pepper. Place cucumber slices and onion rings in a salad bowl, then pour the dressing over them. Toss together and chill until serving.

*Serves 4*

$1/_2$ cup apple cider vinegar

3 cloves garlic, minced

Freshly ground black pepper

2–3 cucumbers, thinly sliced to make about 2 cups

1 small purple onion, thinly sliced and separated into rings

## Tomato-Basil Soup with Garlic Crema Swirl

xxxxxx

*Serves 6*

1 large can (about 28 ounces) crushed tomatoes

3 cloves garlic

1 onion, trimmed, peeled, and roughly chopped

1/2 cup packed fresh basil leaves

1 cup *crema* (Mexican-style sour cream)

6 cloves roasted garlic, removed from skin and mashed (see page 13)

4 cups heavy or whipping cream

Kosher or sea salt

Freshly ground black pepper

*This one's for my husband, who loves the tomato-basil soup at our local faux French bakery-café. It's warm and filling in the winter, yet fresh and tomato-y in the summer. Serve it with slices of crusty French bread that you've toasted and brushed with garlic oil (see page 14).*

In a soup pot over medium-high heat, place the tomatoes, garlic, onion, and basil leaves. Bring to a boil, then turn down the heat and let it simmer for about 30 minutes.

In a small bowl, mix the *crema* and roasted garlic until the mixture is smooth. Set aside.

Transfer the tomato mixture to a food processor or blender and puree. Return it to the soup pot, add cream, and warm gently. Do not allow soup to boil. Season with salt and pepper. Ladle soup into serving bowls, then drizzle each serving with garlic *crema*.

# Zesty Gazpacho

xxxxxx

*This is the equivalent of liquid salad—and because the soup is not cooked, the quality of the ingredients that go into it is the deciding factor on whether the final product is delicious or just okay. To achieve the best texture, make sure to cut all the vegetables the same size. The result is a colorful confetti in your soup!*

Mix all ingredients in a large container that has a lid. Let it chill in the refrigerator for at least 1 day before serving. Taste and adjust seasoning as needed.

This soup keeps well for a week in the refrigerator.

*Serves 8*

2 quarts vegetable juice cocktail or tomato juice

1 cucumber, peeled and finely diced

1 medium purple onion, peeled and finely diced

1 yellow bell pepper, stem and seeds discarded, finely diced

4 garlic cloves, minced

Juice of 2 limes

1/4 cup red wine vinegar

2 tablespoons extra-virgin olive oil

1 tablespoon Worcestershire or soy sauce

1/4 teaspoon Tabasco

Freshly ground black pepper

## Corn Bisque with Garlic and Chiles

xxxxxx

*Serves 4*

2 tablespoons
unsalted butter

1 cup chopped
yellow onions

4 cloves garlic, minced

1/2 cup chopped green chile

1/4 cup diced carrot

1/4 cup diced celery

1/4 cup diced red bell pepper

4 cups fresh or frozen corn
kernels, thawed and drained
(about 42 ounces)

1/4 teaspoon cayenne pepper

3 cups chicken stock

1/2 cup half-and-half or
whole milk

Freshly ground black
pepper

Salt

*I don't know what I love more—making soup or eating it, but either way this is one of my all-time favorites. Feel free to add your own touch, whether it's celery or a variety of chiles. It's a versatile recipe that responds well to experimentation.*

Melt the butter in a large saucepan over medium-high heat. Add onions, garlic, chile, carrot, celery, and red bell pepper, and sauté for about 3 minutes. Add 3 cups of the corn and the cayenne pepper, and sauté another 2 minutes or so. Add stock and bring the mixture to a boil. Reduce heat to medium-low and simmer uncovered until the vegetables are tender and the liquid is slightly reduced, about 30 minutes.

Working in batches, puree the soup in a blender (or use a stick blender). Return the soup to the pot. Mix in half-and-half and the remaining cup of corn. Season to taste with salt and pepper.

This can be prepared a day ahead. Cover and refrigerate. Reheat before serving.

*Entrées*

### Roasted-Garlic–Roasted Chicken

xxxxxx

*Serves 4*

**1 whole chicken (3–4 pounds)**

**1 head roasted garlic, removed from skins and mashed (see page 13)**

**2–3 tablespoons olive oil**

**Salt**

**Freshly ground black pepper**

*Everyone needs a great basic roasted chicken recipe, and this is mine. Not only is it good as is, it also works great for leftovers. Remove the meat from the bones, then use it in chicken salad, quesadillas, and casseroles. I freeze the bones to save for when I have time to simmer a stock.*

Preheat the oven to 400 degrees F.

Rinse the chicken under running water. Remove the giblets and neck from inside the cavity and discard them. Pat the chicken dry with paper towels. Starting at the larger end of the chicken, separate the skin from the breast meat using your hands. You will create two pockets. Spread the garlic over both breasts in the pockets you've just made.

Rub the olive oil over the entire outside of the chicken, then sprinkle generously with salt and pepper. Place the bird in a baking pan and place it in the oven.

After 15 minutes, turn heat down to 325 degrees F and baste the chicken with the juices that have formed in the pan. Bake, basting occasionally, for an additional 35–45 minutes, or until an instant-read thermometer, inserted into the thigh but not touching a bone, reads 180 degrees F.

Remove from the oven and place on a serving platter. Let it rest for at least 5 minutes before slicing to serve.

# Grilled Chicken with Garlic-Chipotle Barbecue Sauce

xxxxxx

*The barbecue sauce can be made several days ahead and stored in the refrigerator until you're ready to grill. Make sure to brush it on only during the last 5 minutes or so of grilling so it doesn't cause flare-ups and burn the chicken. Customize the sauce by replacing the water with fruit juice, wine, or even soda. (Texans love Dr Pepper in everything!)*

In a medium saucepan, mix together ketchup, water, vinegar, garlic, onion, lime juice, brown sugar, Worcestershire sauce, Tabasco, and pepper, and heat the mixture to a boil. Lower the heat and simmer for about 10 minutes. Strain out the solids and discard them.

Prepare and heat the grill. Season the chicken with salt and pepper. When the grill is hot, place the chicken breasts on it, skin side down.

You can also try the sauce on steaks, as a sandwich topping, or as a dipping sauce for chicken nuggets—it makes a great all-around barbecue sauce.

*Serves 4*

$3/4$ cup ketchup

$1/2$ cup water

$1/4$ cup apple cider vinegar

5 garlic cloves, crushed

$1/2$ yellow or white onion, chopped

Juice of 1 lime

3 tablespoons dark brown sugar

1 tablespoon Worcestershire sauce

1 teaspoon chipotle-flavored Tabasco sauce, or more to taste

1 teaspoon freshly ground black pepper, or more to taste

4 large skin-on chicken breasts

Kosher or sea salt

Freshly ground black pepper

## Chicken Enchiladas with Chile-Garlic Sauce

xxxxxx

*Makes 4 servings*

3 tablespoons vegetable oil

1 large onion, chopped

3 cloves garlic, minced

2 tablespoons all-purpose flour

2 cups chopped roasted green chile

2 cups chicken stock

1 teaspoon salt

$1/2$ cup canola or other vegetable oil

1 dozen corn tortillas

Cooking spray

3 cups cooked chicken, shredded or diced

2 cups shredded cheese, Monterey Jack or Cheddar, or a combination

*For a long time, enchiladas were strictly a restaurant food in our family. Then I learned the secret of great enchiladas from a Mexican chef-instructor: the corn tortillas must be softened in hot oil and drained so they don't fall apart in the casserole. It was a revelation to me, and now I love to make enchiladas.*

Heat a heavy saucepan and add the 3 tablespoons of oil. Add the onion and sauté until softened, about 5 minutes. Stir in the garlic and sauté for an additional minute, then add flour and continue cooking for another 2 minutes or so. Mix in the chile, pour in the stock, and add the salt. Bring the mixture to a boil. Reduce heat to a low simmer and cook for about 15 minutes. It will thicken slightly. Remove from heat and set aside.

Heat the ½ cup of oil in a skillet over medium heat. Fry the tortillas, 1 at a time, in the oil for about 15 seconds each. Turn them over with tongs, then cook for another 15 seconds. Drain the prepared tortillas on paper towels.

Preheat the oven to 375 degrees F.

Prepare a baking dish by coating it with cooking spray. With one hand, hold a tortilla. With the other hand, place a row of chicken (a scant ¼ cup) in the center of the tortilla. Top with some shredded cheese. Roll up the tortilla and place it, seam-side down, in the baking pan. Repeat with the remaining tortillas and filling (reserving some of the shredded cheese for topping the enchiladas before baking them).

Pour the prepared garlic-chile sauce over the enchiladas and sprinkle with the remaining shredded cheese. Place in the oven and bake until the cheese is melted and the sauce bubbly, about 25–30 minutes.

*Note:* The sauce keeps, refrigerated, for about 5 days, or you can freeze it for longer storage. You can prepare the casserole ahead of time, wrap well, and refrigerate or freeze it. Bring to room temperature, then bake as directed above.

### Garlic-Pomegranate–Glazed Turkey Breast

xxxxx

*Serves 2*

1 cup pomegranate juice

6 cloves garlic, pressed or minced

¼ cup chopped onion

1 pepper from a can of chipotles in adobo sauce, chopped

1 teaspoon adobo sauce

4 tablespoons unsalted butter

Cooking spray (optional)

1 split bone-in turkey breast, about 2 pounds

¼ teaspoon freshly ground black pepper, or to taste

¼ teaspoon kosher or sea salt, or to taste

*Pomegranate juice is being touted for its anti-oxidant qualities (think cancer-fighters), but it's also delicious and now readily available in supermarkets. Combine it with garlic, and you get a one–two punch of health benefits and great taste. Try this glaze on other poultry, pork, or game—the bold flavors will stand up well to many types of meat.*

In a small saucepan over medium heat, stir together the pomegranate juice, garlic, onion, and chipotle pepper. Heat until the mixture begins to boil, then reduce the heat and simmer for about 10 minutes. Strain, pressing the solids to extract as much liquid as possible. You should have about ¼ cup of liquid remaining. Discard the solids, add the adobo sauce and butter, and heat the mixture just until the butter is melted.

Preheat the oven to 350 degrees F.

Line a roasting pan with foil (shiny side up) or coat it with nonstick cooking spray. Pepper and salt the turkey breast, then place it on a wire rack in the roasting pan. With a pastry brush, coat the turkey breast with the prepared pomegranate-garlic glaze. Place it in oven, basting about every 10–15 minutes, until the turkey is done. It will take about 40 minutes, or until an instant-read thermometer reads 180 degrees F when inserted into the thickest part of the breast.

# Grilled Steaks with Dry Garlic Rub

xxxxxx

*This dry rub is delicious on any cut of beef. Unlike wet marinades, there's no need to coat the meat ahead of time. This recipe makes a scant ¼ cup, but it can be doubled or tripled and kept in your spice cabinet for six months or so. I've even made up large batches and divided it up into glass spice jars to give as holiday gifts, calling it my "Cowgirl Steak and Barbecue Rub." Do make sure to used granulated garlic, which I think is superior to garlic powder or garlic salt.*

*Serves 4*

1 teaspoon ground coffee

1 tablespoon brown sugar

¼ teaspoon cayenne pepper

¼ teaspoon sweet paprika

1 teaspoon granulated garlic

½ teaspoon freshly ground black pepper

½ teaspoon kosher or sea salt

4 boneless sirloin or rib-eye steaks, about 6 ounces each

Mix the coffee, brown sugar, cayenne, paprika, granulated garlic, pepper, and salt in a small bowl. Heat a gas or charcoal grill to medium-high heat.

Pat dry rub on each steak. Place the steaks on the grill and cook for about 5 minutes on the first side, then turn them over and cook for another 3–5 minutes, depending upon the thickness of the meat. When done, an instant-read thermometer will read 145 degrees F for medium-rare or 160 for medium.

## Southwestern Stir-fry

xxxxxx

*Serves 4*

1 tablespoon olive
or vegetable oil

1 pound sirloin steak,
cut into strips about
1/2 x 4 inches

Salt

Freshly ground pepper

1 onion, cut into
thin wedges

1 red bell pepper,
cut into thin wedges

2 garlic cloves, thinly sliced

4 green onions,
trimmed and thinly sliced

Flour tortillas, warmed

Salsa

Sour cream

*This recipe is kind of like fajitas, but faster and easier. If you have time, you could marinate the meat ahead of time in Worcestershire sauce, lime juice, and a little cumin. Don't hesitate to toss in any seasonal vegetable—just make sure to cut everything the same size so it all cooks at the same rate. That's the secret to successful stir-fry.*

Heat the oil in a large skillet over high heat until the oil shimmers but isn't smoking. Season the beef strips with salt and pepper and add them to the hot oil, tossing to coat. Add the onion wedges, bell pepper, and garlic, and cook for about 4–5 minutes or until the beef is cooked through and the vegetables are just starting to wilt. Remove from heat and toss in the green onions.

Serve the stir-fry with tortillas, salsa, and sour cream.

## Beef Kebabs with
## Mango-Garlic-Chile Marinade

xxxxx

*Makes 6 servings*

2 pounds boneless
top sirloin

½ cup mango nectar
(jarred or canned)

4 cloves garlic, minced

1 teaspoon crushed
red chile

1 tablespoon olive oil

*Food on a stick always says "party" to me. I love making all kinds of kebabs for the grill, whether with meat or vegetables or some combination of the two. Just make sure to soak the skewers in water for about 30 minutes so they don't catch on fire.*

Cut the beef into 2 x 1-inch cubes.

Place beef cubes, mango nectar, garlic, red chile, and olive oil in a gallon-size plastic zipper bag. Refrigerate at least 2 hours or overnight.

Prepare the grill or preheat the broiler.

Remove the beef cubes from the marinade and place them on skewers. Place them on the preheated grill, or on a roasting pan under the broiler. Cook for about 5 minutes on one side, basting with some of the remaining marinade. Turn over and cook for another 3–5 minutes, or until the meat is cooked through.

# Double Garlic Meat Loaf

xxxxxx

*This meat loaf benefits from the kick of sautéed garlic and the richness of roasted garlic. When sautéing vegetables, it's easy to burn tiny pieces of minced garlic over high heat. Instead, add it near the end of the cooking period or simply sauté it whole, then mash with a fork as demonstrated in this recipe.*

Preheat the oven to 375 degrees F.

Melt butter in a heavy medium-size skillet over medium-low heat. Add onion, bell pepper, and garlic cloves. Season with salt, pepper, cayenne, oregano, and cumin. Cook, stirring frequently, until the onions are transparent and the bell pepper is tender, about 10 minutes. Mash the garlic cloves with a fork.

In a large bowl, combine the ground meat, beaten eggs, bread crumbs, green chile, mashed roasted garlic, ketchup, and Worcestershire sauce. Stir in the onion mixture and mix well.

Pack the meat loaf mixture into the cups of a muffin tin (regular-size or miniature, depending on how large or small you want your meat loaves). Bake for 20–25 minutes until cooked through. Drain the fat, if any, from the tin, remove the mini-loaves, and serve hot.

For 1 large loaf, pack the mixture into a loaf pan and bake 50–60 minutes. Pour off the fat from the pan and let the meat loaf rest for 10 minutes. Remove from the pan, then slice and serve.

This makes a superb filling for tamales or *chiles rellenos*.

*Serves 6–8*

4 tablespoons unsalted butter or canola oil

2 cups finely chopped onion (about 2 medium)

1/2 cup finely chopped red bell pepper

4 cloves garlic

2 teaspoons salt

1 teaspoon freshly ground black pepper

1 teaspoon cayenne pepper

1 teaspoon oregano

1/2 teaspoon ground cumin

2 pounds meat loaf mix: equal parts lean ground beef, ground pork, and ground veal

2 large eggs, lightly beaten in a small bowl

1 cup unseasoned bread crumbs

1/2 cup finely chopped roasted mild green chile

1 head roasted garlic, removed from skins and mashed

1/2 cup ketchup

2 teaspoons Worcestershire sauce

## Pork Loin with Garlic-Honey Glaze

xxxxxx

*Serves 6*

**Cooking spray (optional)**

**1 center-cut pork loin filet, or 2 pork tenderloins, about 1³/₄ pounds total**

**¹/₄ cup honey**

**1 tablespoon dark soy sauce**

**6 cloves garlic, minced or pressed**

**1 teaspoon freshly ground black pepper**

**Pinch of salt**

*This dish has an Asian accent, which is fitting because China produces the most garlic of any country in the world, and the Chinese use it prodigiously in their food and as medicine. Garlic use goes back centuries in Asia.*

Preheat the oven to 375 degrees F.

Prepare a baking pan by coating it with cooking spray or lining it with aluminum foil, shiny side up. Place the pork on the prepared pan.

Mix honey, soy sauce, garlic, pepper, and salt in a small bowl or liquid measuring cup. Pour about half the mixture over the pork roast. Place in the oven and bake. After about 20 minutes, remove the roast from the oven and pour the remaining honey mixture over the roast. Return roast to the oven and continue to cook, about 20–30 minutes more, until an instant-read thermometer measures 160 degrees F when inserted into the center of the roast.

Let the roast stand for about 10 minutes before slicing.

# Grilled Fish with Roasted Tomato and Garlic Sauce

xxxxxx

*This recipe was the surprise hit of a class I taught on Hatch chiles. I used fresh golden trout, though snapper or any other mild fish would work well. Keeping the fish whole, as opposed to cutting it into fillets, help keeps the fish moist and tender on the grill. It takes a few minutes longer to cook, but it's worth the wait.*

Preheat the oven to 425 degrees F.

Line a baking sheet with parchment paper or aluminum foil. Place the tomatoes, onion, chiles, and garlic on the pan and place it in the oven. Roast, turning the vegetables several times, for about 15–20 minutes, until they are soft and beginning to brown. Set aside to cool.

When the tomatoes and chiles are cool enough to handle, remove the cores, seeds, and skins. In a food processor or blender, pulse the roasted vegetables until a chunky sauce is formed. Add the cilantro, parsley, and salt. Set aside.

Prepare a gas or charcoal grill and heat to medium to medium-hot. Check the fish for any remaining scales and remove them as needed. Rinse well under running water and pat dry with paper towels. Rub the fish with oil, then sprinkle all over and inside with oregano, salt, and pepper.

Place the fish directly on the preheated grill. Cook for about 6 minutes, then turn and cook another 6 minutes. When done,

*Serves 4*

2 pounds ripe tomatoes

1 yellow or white onion, trimmed, peeled, and quartered

2 green chiles, preferably Hatch

8 cloves garlic

1/4 cup fresh cilantro leaves, stems removed

3 tablespoons fresh flat-leaf parsley leaves, stems removed

1 1/2 teaspoons kosher salt, or more to taste

1 whole, mild fish (3–4 pounds), head and scales removed, butterflied

1/4 cup canola or olive oil

1–2 teaspoons oregano

Salt

Freshly ground black pepper

Lime wedges

the fish will be flaky and opaque in the center—you can test it with a small paring knife.

Serve the fish with the prepared tomato sauce and lime wedges. The sauce can be made a few days ahead and refrigerated. Bring it to room temperature before serving with fish.

## Roasted Garlic–Green Chile Macaroni and Cheese

xxxxxx

*Serves 6–8*

1 pound elbow macaroni or other small tubular pasta

1 tablespoon unsalted butter

1 tablespoon all-purpose flour

1 1/2 cups whole milk

4 ounces cream cheese

2 cups shredded sharp Cheddar cheese, or a combination of Cheddar and Monterey Jack

1 head roasted garlic (see page 13), removed from skins and mashed

1/4 teaspoon kosher or sea salt

1/2 teaspoon ground white pepper (or black pepper if you don't mind the dark specks)

2 roasted green chiles, peeled and chopped, or 1 can (4 ounces) mild peeled Hatch green chiles

*Homemade macaroni and cheese is one of the greatest comfort foods ever invented. The sauce can be made in the same amount of time it takes to cook the noodles, so it doesn't necessarily take longer to make than the boxed stuff. Experiment with various types of cheeses to vary the taste.*

Cook the macaroni or other pasta according to the package directions, making sure to salt the water.

In a medium saucepan over medium heat, melt the butter. Stir in the flour and cook, stirring constantly, for about 3–4 minutes. Do not let the mixture brown. If it does, rinse out the pan and start over. (If it's too dark, it won't thicken the cheese sauce.)

Whisk in the milk, then add the cream cheese and shredded cheese. Let the cheese melt, but do not let the mixture boil. Stir in the mashed roasted garlic, and season with pepper and salt.

Drain the pasta and add it to the sauce. Carefully stir in the chiles. Serve hot.

# Linguine with Roasted Tomato and Garlic Sauce

XXXXXX

*My friend Linda, who learned to cook from her Italian grandmother, taught me the importance of salting water for pasta. "It should be as salty as the sea," she says. I love this sauce at room temperature instead of piping hot. At the table, pass grated Parmigiano-Reggiano cheese and crushed red peppers to season to taste.*

Preheat the oven to 425 degrees F.

Line a shallow-rimmed baking pan (like a jellyroll pan) with aluminum foil or coat it with cooking spray. Place the tomatoes, garlic, and onion on the pan, drizzle them with olive oil, and sprinkle with salt and pepper. Place the pan into the hot oven and roast for about 30 minutes, turning everything after the first 15 minutes.

Meanwhile, cook the pasta according to the package directions.

Remove the vegetables from the oven and set them aside. When the tomatoes are cool enough to handle, slip off their skins. Place the tomatoes, garlic, and onion in a food processor fitted with a metal blade or in a blender. Pulse a few times until a chunky sauce is formed. Tear the basil leaves right before serving and stir them into the sauce.

Reheat the sauce, if desired, or serve at room temperature with linguine.

*Serves 4*

Cooking spray (optional)

12 Roma tomatoes, cored

1 head garlic, cloves separated and peeled

1 large yellow or white onion, trimmed, peeled, and cut into wedges

3–4 tablespoons olive oil

1/2 teaspoon kosher or sea salt

1 teaspoon freshly ground black pepper

1 pound linguine, fresh or dried

1/4 cup fresh basil leaves

## Grilled Portobello Mushrooms with Garlic Oil

xxxxxx

*Serves 6*

**6 portobello mushroom caps, stems trimmed**

**1/4 cup garlic oil (see page 14)**

*Portobello mushrooms are meaty enough to grill—and to stand in as an entrée. Clean by wiping with paper towels or a vegetable brush, because rinsing or submerging them will cause them to absorb too much water, and they will be soggy and taste steamed.*

Prepare a charcoal or gas grill, or a grill pan. Brush the mushrooms on both sides with garlic oil. Over medium-high heat, place the mushroom caps, top side down, directly on the grate. Let them cook for about 5 minutes, then turn them over. Baste with additional garlic oil. Cook for another 2–3 minutes, then remove from heat.

These mushrooms are especially good when served atop a bed of well-seasoned risotto or couscous.

# Fusilli with Sausage in Sun-Dried Tomato–Garlic Cream Sauce

xxxxxx

*Serve this entrée with a green salad for a quick weeknight meal. Because this recipe calls for relatively few ingredients, don't hesitate to splurge on a wedge of aged Parmigiano-Reggiano cheese to grate over the dish. The flavor is worlds away from the powdery stuff sold in cans.*

Heat the oil in a large heavy skillet over medium-high heat. Add the sausage, sun-dried tomatoes, and garlic. Cook, stirring frequently, until the sausage is lightly browned. Drain the mixture in a colander, then return it to the pan.

Add the sage, Marsala or vermouth, and broth to the pan. Cook, stirring, until the mixture is reduced by about half and thickened. Add the cream and cook for about 5 minutes, but do not let the sauce come to a boil.

Add the fusilli and stir just until heated. Add the cheese, then salt and pepper to taste and serve immediately.

*Serves 2–3*

1 tablespoon olive oil

12 ounces pork sausage (hot or mild), removed from casing and crumbled

5 oil-packed sun-dried tomato halves, thinly sliced

6 cloves garlic, trimmed and thinly sliced

2 teaspoons fresh sage leaves (or 1 teaspoon dried)

$1/4$ cup Marsala wine or sweet red vermouth

$1/3$ cup chicken broth

$1/4$–$1/2$ cup heavy cream

8 ounces fusilli pasta, cooked and drained

$1/4$ cup grated Parmigiano-Reggiano cheese

Salt

Freshly ground black pepper

## Roasted Garlic Pork Soft Tacos

xxxxxx

*Serves 4*

Cooking spray (optional)

1 bone-in pork roast (Boston butt)

Salt

Freshly ground black pepper

1 head garlic, cloves peeled and separated

2 tablespoons vegetable oil

2 large onions, chopped

1 cup chopped fresh cilantro leaves (stems removed)

12 corn tortillas, warmed

1 bunch green onions, chopped, green parts only

Lime wedges, for garnish

Salsa, sour cream, and chopped tomatoes, optional

*Boston butt is a highly flavorful cut of pork. This recipe is a good project for the weekend, when most of us have a little more time to slow-roast the meat, then package portions for weeknight meals. The cooked meat keeps well in the freezer when wrapped securely in plastic or foil.*

Preheat the oven to 350 degrees F. Place the pork roast on a baking sheet that has been coated with cooking spray or lined with aluminum foil; sprinkle with salt and pepper. With a thin-bladed knife, cut small slits in various depths all over the roast. Insert 1 clove of garlic into each slit. Roast the pork until it is brown and very tender, about 2 hours. Cool. Shred the pork, discarding the bone and fat.

Heat the oil in a large skillet over medium-high heat. Add the onions and sauté until tender, about 10 minutes. Add the shredded pork and cilantro; stir until heated through. Season with salt and pepper.

Arrange warm tortillas on plates or a serving platter. Top each with pork and sprinkle with green onions. Serve with lime wedges and, if desired, salsa, sour cream, and chopped tomatoes.

# Grilled Corn with Garlic-Lime Butter

xxxxxx

*Grilling corn in the husk allows it to steam gently on the grill and takes about 10 to 15 minutes over medium heat. Shucking the corn first makes it a bit quicker to cook—maybe 8 to 10 minutes, total—and gives it a smokier flavor and allows some of the kernels to char. Either way is delicious, but you've got to keep a closer eye on shucked corn so it doesn't burn too much.*

While the corn is cooking, place the butter, garlic, lime juice, pepper, and salt in a small saucepan and heat, stirring until the butter is melted and all ingredients are combined. As soon as the corn is cooked, brush the butter mixture over each ear and reserve any leftover mixture for passing at the table.

For extra citrus zing, add the zest from the lime to the mixture.

*Serves 4–6*

**4 ears grilled fresh corn**

**4 tablespoons unsalted butter**

**4 cloves garlic, minced or pressed**

**Juice of 1 lime**

**1 teaspoon freshly ground black pepper**

**$1/2$ teaspoon kosher or sea salt**

## Garlic Potatoes Anna

xxxxxx

*Serves 6–8*

6 tablespoons softened unsalted butter, divided

2 pounds potatoes, sliced paper thin

1 head roasted garlic (see page 13), removed from skin and mashed

Salt

Freshly ground black pepper

*This variation of a classic dish highlights the flavor of roasted garlic. Garlic infuses the potatoes during baking, making this a more elegant side dish than its homey cousin, roasted garlic mashed potatoes. It helps to have a mandolin to cut the potato slices paper-thin, but a food processor's fine slicing blade also works. Otherwise, get out a chef's knife and your patience.*

Preheat the oven to 350 degrees F.

Coat a 2-quart ovenproof casserole dish with about 2 tablespoons of butter. Place one layer of potatoes on the bottom of the dish. Dot with more butter and bits of roasted garlic, then top with a layer of potatoes. Repeat until you have used all of the potatoes, garlic, and butter. Cover the dish with aluminum foil.

Place the casserole dish in the oven and bake for 20 minutes. Uncover the dish and continue baking for about 1 hour. Potatoes are done when the tip of a knife can be inserted easily into the middle of the casserole. Serve hot with salt and pepper.

# Roasted Garlic Mashed Potatoes

xxxxxx

*Cream cheese and sour cream are added to the potatoes to add richness, but also to help them retain their texture when reheated. I usually make this recipe the day before serving in much larger quantities: 10 pounds of potatoes for a big family dinner, 20 pounds when I used to bring this dish to the office Thanksgiving potluck.*

Boil the potatoes in salted water until tender, about 15 minutes. Drain and place them in a large mixing bowl. Add the butter, cream or milk, cream cheese, sour cream, and roasted garlic. Mix everything together with a potato masher for slightly chunky, home-style mashed potatoes. For ultra-smooth potatoes, use an electric mixer.

Season with salt and pepper to taste. Serve hot.

Store any leftovers in a covered container in the refrigerator. You can reheat them in a microwave or, covered with aluminum foil, in a 350-degree F oven until hot.

*Serves 8*

3 pounds Idaho potatoes, peeled and cut into large chunks

Salt

8 tablespoons (1 stick) unsalted butter, softened

1/2 cup heavy cream or whole milk

4 ounces cream cheese, brought to room temperature

1/2 cup sour cream

1 head roasted garlic, removed from skin and mashed (see page 13)

Salt

Freshly ground black pepper

## Garlic Couscous

xxxxxx

*Serves 4*

1 cup water

¼ teaspoon salt,
or more to taste

1 tablespoon butter

1 cup couscous

1 tablespoon
toasted minced garlic
(see page 14)

*Couscous is a tiny, granular pasta of Moroccan origin. It's remarkably versatile—able to absorb any and all flavors and to stand in for potatoes or rice. Most grocery stores stock it with the grains and rice or in the pasta aisle. New variations are available, including a tri-color blend enhanced with tomato and spinach.*

Bring the water, salt, and butter to a boil in a saucepan. Add the couscous and toasted garlic and stir. Remove the pan from heat, cover, and let stand for 5 minutes. Fluff with a fork and serve.

This is especially good with the Shrimp Mojo de Ajo (see page 24), or with Grilled Portobello Mushrooms (see page 52).

## Cilantro-Garlic Rice

xxxxxx

*Cilantro has a distinctive flavor profile that people seem to either love or hate. Some unfortunate souls have taste buds that can detect only a soapy taste when they eat the leaves. To showcase cilantro's bright, herbal characteristics, stir it into the cooked rice.*

You'll need a large saucepan with a tight-fitting lid. Place the pan over medium or medium-high heat. Add the oil. When the oil begins to shimmer (don't let it smoke—then it's too hot), add the rice and sauté until golden brown and fragrant.

Add the tomato sauce, water, bouillon cubes, garlic, and oregano, and stir well. Lower the heat to medium-low and cover the pan.

Do not stir the rice. Allow it to cook for 20 minutes, or until all the liquid has been absorbed. Turn off the heat and let it rest. Just before serving, stir the cilantro into the rice.

*Serves 8*

4 tablespoons olive or vegetable oil

2 cups long-grain white rice

1 1/2 cups canned tomato sauce

4 cups water

4 chicken bouillon cubes, crushed

4 cloves garlic, trimmed and minced

1 tablespoon oregano

1/4 cup cilantro leaves, stems removed

## Garlic Pinto Beans

xxxxxx

*Serves 6–8*

1 pound pinto beans

1 quart water

1 can or bottle of beer

½ pound bacon, chopped (optional)

2 jalapeño peppers, stems removed, chopped

1 yellow onion, peeled and chopped

¼ cup chopped cilantro

1 small tomato, chopped

4 cloves garlic, peeled and chopped

1 teaspoon ground black pepper, or more to taste

1 teaspoon salt, or more to taste (optional if using bacon)

*To cook beans faster, you'll need to pick through and soak the beans overnight in enough water to cover them. Rinse in a colander, then prepare as recipe directs. Beans should be ready in about half the time it takes to cook them without soaking.*

Rinse the beans and sort them to remove any small stones or other debris.

Combine all ingredients in a large stock pot and bring to a boil. Reduce the heat and simmer for 2–3 hours, until the beans are tender. Add more water during cooking if necessary.

## Sautéed Summer Squash
## with Sweet Onions and Garlic

xxxxxx

*Squash serves as the perfect foil for the culinary cousins—garlic and onion—in this recipe. For sweet onions, look for the names 1015, Walla Walla, Maui, or Vidalia. If these are not in season, try a sweet yellow or purple onion for the best flavor.*

Place the pan over medium-high heat and add the oil. Sauté the onions for 3–4 minutes or until they are softened and clear. Add the garlic and stir, cooking for about 1 minute. Add the squash, then turn the heat down to medium. Stir frequently for 4–5 minutes or until the squash is tender. Season with salt and pepper, then add butter and serve while hot.

*Makes 4 servings*

1 tablespoon olive oil

1 small sweet onion, sliced thinly

2 cloves garlic, trimmed and chopped

2 cups sliced yellow crookneck squash, sliced about ⅛ inch thick

Salt

Freshly ground pepper

1 tablespoon unsalted butter

## Garlic Roasted Asparagus with Orange Zest

xxxxxx

*Serves 6*

Cooking spray (optional)

1 pound asparagus, trimmed

2 tablespoons olive oil

6 cloves garlic, minced or pressed

Shredded peel from 1 large navel orange

*Zest is the colored part of the fruit rind that contains flavorful and aromatic citrus oil. The best way to remove the zest without getting any of the underlying bitter white membrane is with a Microplane grater or a citrus zester, or by rubbing the fruit over the fine holes of a box grater, being careful not to include any of the pith.*

Preheat the oven to 425 degrees F.

Prepare a jellyroll pan or a rimmed cookie sheet by coating it with nonstick baking spray, or line the pan with parchment paper.

Place the asparagus on the prepared pan and drizzle it with olive oil. Sprinkle it evenly with garlic and shredded orange peel. Place the pan in the oven and bake for 5 minutes. Remove the pan from the oven and roll the asparagus over, using tongs. Return the pan to the oven and bake until done, about 3–5 minutes. The asparagus will be tender and just beginning to darken.

## Zucchini with Garlic and Cherry Tomatoes

xxxxxx

*Serves 4*

Cooking spray (optional)

2 zucchini, sliced into $1/4$-inch rounds

1 cup cherry tomatoes

1 medium onion, sliced horizontally and separated into rings

4 cloves garlic

2 tablespoons olive or vegetable oil

$1/2$ teaspoon dried oregano, or 1 teaspoon chopped fresh

$1/4$ teaspoon dried thyme, or $1/2$ teaspoon chopped fresh

$1/4$ cup grated Parmigiano-Reggiano cheese

*Roasting vegetables really ups the flavor ante. Their natural sugars condense and caramelize, with the result being a tender, delicious dish. Of course, this recipe also works well with summer squash instead of zucchini, or a combination of the two.*

Preheat the oven to 425 degrees F.

Coat a jellyroll pan or other shallow-edged baking pan with cooking spray, or line it with aluminum foil or parchment paper. Place the zucchini, tomatoes, onion, and garlic on the pan. Drizzle them with oil, then sprinkle with oregano and thyme.

Roast the vegetables in the oven for about 7 minutes. Remove from the oven and toss, then return and roast for about 5 minutes more.

Sprinkle with cheese and serve hot.

# Triple-Lily Risotto

xxxxxx

*The three lilies in this recipe are the onion, shallots, and garlic, all members of the same botanical family. This versatile recipe works well as a side dish or as an entrée. I like to add a pound of shelled, deveined medium shrimp along with the cheese at the end of the cooking. Gently stir in the shrimp and cover the pan. The steam will cook the shrimp in about 3 minutes or so.*

*Serves 6*

6–8 cups chicken stock

2 tablespoons olive oil

1 medium onion, chopped

2 large shallots, minced

6 cloves garlic, minced

3 tablespoons unsalted butter

1 1/2 cups arborio rice

1/2 cup grated Parmigiano-Reggiano cheese

1/4 cup chopped flat-leaf parsley

Freshly ground black pepper

Salt

Warm up the chicken stock in a medium saucepan and keep it at a simmer on the stove.

Heat a large saucepan over medium heat. Add the olive oil, onion, shallots, and garlic. Sauté for about 3–5 minutes, or until the vegetables are softened. Add butter and rice, stirring until the rice just starts to brown.

Add about 1 cup of the warm chicken stock to the rice mixture and stir well. As soon as the stock is absorbed into the rice, add another cup. Continue this process until the rice is thick, creamy, and cooked through. It should take about 40–50 minutes. Remove from heat and stir in the cheese and parsley. Season with black pepper and salt to taste.

*Variation* This dish is also wonderful when served the next day as a "risotto cake." Butter a 10-inch round springform pan and dust it with seasoned bread crumbs. Fill the pan with the warm risotto mixture and pack it firmly. Cover with aluminum foil and refrigerate overnight. The next day, preheat the oven to 350 degrees F. Place the covered pan in the oven and bake until the risotto is heated through, about 50 minutes.

Remove the pan from the oven and discard the aluminum foil. Sprinkle the top of the cake with about ¼ cup of shredded Parmigiano-Reggiano cheese and return it to the oven until the cheese is melted. To serve, remove the springform ring from the pan, then cut the rice cake into wedges.

## Garlic Focaccia

xxxxx

*Serves 4*

1½ cups warm water, 105–115 degrees F

1 package (¼ ounce) active dry yeast

1 teaspoon honey

4 cups all-purpose flour

½ teaspoon salt

2 teaspoons oregano

4 garlic cloves, pressed

2 tablespoons olive oil, divided, plus more for coating the pan

Pinch of kosher or coarse sea salt

¼ cup grated Parmigiano-Reggiano cheese

*This dough can be patted out into a rectangle about 11 by 15 inches, or rolled thin like a cracker. The absolute best crust is formed when you use a preheated baking stone in a very hot oven. This is the bread to use for panini sandwiches—just slice in half horizontally, fill with roasted vegetables or cold cuts and cheese, then toast like a grilled cheese sandwich. It's a great way to use one of those popular electric indoor grills.*

In a 2-cup mixing cup, measure the warm water, then add the yeast and honey. Stir and set aside.

In the bowl of a stand mixer fitted with the dough hook, mix the flour, salt, oregano, and garlic on low speed, just until combined. Pour in the water, yeast, and honey mixture. Turn the mixer to low again to moisten the ingredients, then turn it to medium-high and knead the dough for 5 minutes. The dough should be fairly slack and slightly sticky to the touch.

Coat a large mixing bowl with 1 tablespoon of olive oil. Oil your hands and scrape the dough out of the mixing bowl, forming it into a rough ball. Place it in the oil-coated bowl and turn it over to coat the dough. Cover with a clean towel and set aside in a warm, draft-free place. Let it rise until doubled, about 1–1½ hours.

Preheat the oven to 450 degrees F.

Turn the dough out onto a large baking pan that has been generously greased with olive oil or lined with parchment paper. Pat out the dough into a rough rectangle, about 10 x 15 inches. Drizzle with the remaining tablespoon of olive oil, then sprinkle with salt and cheese. Let the dough rest about 10–15 minutes while the oven preheats.

Place the pan in the hot oven and bake for about 10–15 minutes, or until the focaccia is golden brown on the outside. Let it cool before cutting and serving.

*Variation*  Experiment with various herbs in the dough and different cheeses for toppings.

## Roasted Garlic French Bread

xxxxxx

*Serves 6–8*

1 package (¼ ounce) active dry yeast

1 teaspoon honey

½ cup water (warmed to 105–115 degrees F)

3–3½ cups unbleached all-purpose flour

1 teaspoon salt

½–¾ cup room-temperature water

2 tablespoons olive oil, divided, plus extra for greasing the bowl

2 heads of roasted garlic (see page 13)

½ cup grated Asiago cheese

2–3 tablespoons finely chopped flat-leaf parsley

*I call this bread my "inside out" garlic bread, because the garlic and cheese show up as a swirl inside the loaf when it's sliced. You can substitute Parmigiano-Reggiano, Romano, or another hard grating cheese for the Asiago.*

Mix the yeast and honey with the warm water in a small bowl or in the measuring cup.

Measure 3 cups of flour into the bowl of a food processor fitted with a metal blade. Add the salt and pulse a few times to mix.

With the machine running, pour in the water-yeast-honey mixture through the feed tube. Drizzle in additional water just until a dough ball forms. The amount of water needed will vary depending upon the condition of the flour and the weather. Add extra flour only if necessary to form a dough ball. Let the machine run for about 1 minute to knead the bread.

Drizzle a tablespoon or so of olive oil into a large bowl. Remove the dough from the processor and shape it into a ball. Place the dough, top-side down, into the bowl, then flip it over to coat with olive oil. Cover the bowl with a piece of plastic wrap and set aside in a warm, draft-free place.

In a small bowl, mix together the roasted garlic and 1 tablespoon of olive oil until it forms a thick paste. Set aside.

Let the dough rise until doubled in size, about 1 hour. Dust a baking pan with flour. Remove the dough from the bowl and press it out onto the baking pan, shaping it into a rectangle. Do not knead the dough or overwork it.

Spread the roasted garlic and olive oil paste over the rectangle. Sprinkle with grated cheese, then with chopped parsley. Roll up the dough like a jellyroll and tuck the two ends under.

Cover the loaf with plastic wrap and set it aside in a warm, draft-free place for 30–45 minutes. Preheat the oven to 400 degrees F.

Remove the plastic wrap from the loaf and, with a serrated knife, slash three or four slits, evenly spaced across the top of the bread. Place the bread on its baking pan in the preheated oven. Bake for about 25–30 minutes, or until an instant-read thermometer reaches 190 degrees F when inserted into the center of the bread.

Let the bread cool completely before slicing.

*Note:* Instead of a food processor, you may use a stand mixer fitted with a bread hook to make the dough, making sure to mix for at least 5 minutes so it will be well kneaded.

## Cheddar-Garlic Biscuits

xxxxxx

*Serves 8*

1 cup all-purpose flour, plus extra for dusting

1 teaspoon sugar

2 teaspoons baking powder

1/4 teaspoon salt

1/4 cup solid shortening

2 cloves roasted garlic, mashed (see page 13)

1/2 cup grated Cheddar cheese

1/3–1/2 cup buttermilk

Cooking spray (optional)

2 tablespoons unsalted butter, melted

*Trying to replicate the biscuits at a popular chain eatery, I studied dozens of recipes. Disappointed by the prevalence of garlic powder and baking mix, I decided to give up and come up with something unique. Raw garlic was too bitter, but roasted worked fine. Don't expect mile-high, fluffy biscuits—these are flaky and rich, just right to serve with dinner or make into tiny, 1-inch rounds to serve with a glass of wine.*

Preheat the oven to 400 degrees F.

In a mixing bowl, combine the flour, sugar, baking powder, and salt. In a small bowl, cream together the shortening and roasted garlic. With two knives, cut the shortening mixture into the dry ingredients until coarse crumbs are formed. Fold in the grated cheese, being careful not to over-mix. Add about 1/3 cup buttermilk and stir just until dry ingredients are moistened, adding a little more buttermilk if necessary.

Turn out the dough onto a lightly floured surface and pat it out into a rough circle about 1/2 inch thick. Cut the dough into biscuits with a round 2-inch cutter and place them on a baking pan that has been coated with cooking spray or lined with parchment paper.

Place them in the oven and bake for about 20 minutes or until tops are golden brown. Remove from the oven and immediately brush with melted butter.

## Cheesy Garlic-Jalapeño Cornbread

xxxxxx

*I can't imagine baking cornbread in anything but one of my well-seasoned hand-me-down cast-iron skillets. The good news is that everyone can have one now, even if they don't have a Southern grandmother in the family tree. New cast-iron skillets can be purchased pre-seasoned, taking some of the work— and years—off that chore.*

Preheat the oven to 350 degrees F.

In a mixing bowl, whisk together the flour, cornmeal, sugar, salt, baking powder, baking soda, garlic, and jalapeño.

Measure the buttermilk into a 2-cup mixing cup. Add the egg and whisk the mixture with a fork.

Place the butter in a 10-inch cast-iron skillet or an 8 x 8-inch baking pan, and put this into the oven until the butter is melted.

Pour the liquid mixture over the dry ingredients in the mixing bowl. Add the grated cheese. Fold the ingredients together with a spatula. Do not over-mix.

Remove the pan from the oven and scrape the cornbread batter in over the butter. Do not stir. Return the pan to the oven and bake for about 30–40 minutes, until the top is golden-brown and the cornbread is cooked through.

*Serves 8*

1 cup all-purpose flour

1 cup yellow cornmeal

1 tablespoon sugar

1 teaspoon salt

2 teaspoons baking powder

$\frac{1}{2}$ teaspoon baking soda

3 cloves garlic, pressed

1 jalapeño, stem removed, seeded, and finely chopped

1 $\frac{1}{2}$ cups buttermilk

1 egg

8 tablespoons (1 stick) unsalted butter

1 cup grated Cheddar cheese

*Equipment*

Here are a few things I can't cook without.

**INSTANT-READ THERMOMETER** No more need to cut into a steak to see if it's done or guess when the Thanksgiving turkey is ready. An instant-read thermometer, available at most supermarkets or kitchen shops starting at about $5, is essential for ensuring food safety and quality.

It's important to locate the thermometer's sensor so you know about how deep to insert the stem for an accurate reading. Look for a little dimple, dent or hole about one-quarter to one-third the way up from the point. That's where you want to test the thickest part of meat or the center of a loaf of bread.

Once you have a thermometer, you need to test its accuracy. It's easy: boil a pot of water and insert the thermometer, making sure the sensor is submerged. The temperature should read 212 degrees F. If it doesn't, you'll need to adjust it by turning the small nut right under the dial with a pair of needle-nose pliers—or remember the difference, and mentally calculate the correct temperature each time you use the thermometer.

**OVEN THERMOMETER** Home ovens are rarely calibrated accurately. Buy an inexpensive oven thermometer—again, less than $5—and at least you'll have an idea about how hot it is in there. None of the recipes in this book demand total accuracy, but it's certainly helpful to be able to predict how long something is going to take to roast or bake.

**KNIVES** "A dull knife is a dangerous knife" is my mantra, especially when I'm teaching knife-skills classes. Dull knives slip, and when they do and your finger gets sliced, it's usually not a clean cut, it heals slowly, and it often leaves a scar.

If you're not into sharpening stones and honing steels, take your knives to a professional once or twice a year. Look in the phone book or inquire at a local fabric store. They often invite in a professional who can sharpen scissors and your knives.

As far as inventory goes, you need only three knives to do most culinary jobs: a chef's knife, a paring knife, and a serrated bread knife. That's all I used to prepare every dish in this book.

**PEPPER GRINDER** Most of the pre-ground stuff sold in little cans and jars in the supermarket might as well be sawdust. Buy whole peppercorns and grind them as you need them. Sure, you can spend $100 on some fancy-schmancy mill, but a $10 model from the discount store works just fine.

## *Ingredients*

APPENDIX II.

I'll start with the same point I make when I teach a cooking class: you cannot make a superior product from inferior ingredients. For best results, use the best quality ingredients you can find. Note that I did not say the most *expensive* ingredients. The best cooks are the most discerning shoppers.

Once you have quality ingredients, treat them with respect. If a recipe calls for room-temperature butter, don't melt it, and don't use it straight from the refrigerator.

Speaking of **BUTTER**, I prefer unsalted butter. It's fresher and the flavor isn't masked by salt. Buy it on sale and store what you're not going to use within a couple of weeks in the freezer, preferably inside a heavy-duty plastic bag or wrapped in foil to keep out odors. My philosophy is that I'd rather have one tea-spoon of real butter than a tub of oily fake stuff, and most health professionals agree.

**OLIVE OIL.** I'm not a brand snob, and I keep only one kind on hand at all times—a decent quality, extra-virgin product that I can use in salad dressing or in a sauté. Olive oil can and will turn rancid, so buy reasonable quantities. If you have excess, store it in your refrigerator. It will turn cloudy and thicken but will return to its usual lovely viscosity at room temperature.

If a recipe calls for **MILK,** I specify the type and acceptable substitute, if any. I generally use whole milk for cooking. If it calls for cream, I look for pasteurized heavy or whipping cream, not "ultrapasteurized."

**GROUND SPICES AND DRIED HERBS** have a limited shelf life, generally no more than one year. Buy what you need in small quantities and write the purchase date on the con-tainer. I know it's difficult to toss out that almost-full jar that cost $3.49, but let go. Always give questionable herbs and spices the sniff test. The nose knows.

**SALT.** I use either coarse kosher salt or fine-grained sea salt, depending on the texture (or lack thereof) and flavor I want in a dish. Unless you are on a salt-restricted diet for health rea-sons, don't leave out the modest amounts of salt in these dishes—but always adjust it to your taste. In some recipes, like the yeast breads, salt plays an important chemical role to keep the leavening in check. I often tell students that one sure way to improve culinary skill immediately is to judiciously use salt and pepper.

**PEPPER.** See "pepper grinder" under Equipment.

**BAKING SODA AND BAKING POWDER.** Make sure they're fresh. Check the expiration dates. If the box is so old it doesn't have an expiration date—well, it's too old. Buy new. Recipes that use either or both these leaveners should be baked as quickly as possible after being mixed to obtain the best results.

**YEAST** is a tiny living organism that is brought back to life when mixed with water and given a little of its favorite food, sugar. Don't fear yeast; modern manufacturing methods have taken almost all the risk out of using it to make baked goods. Check the expiration date and follow the recipe, and you'll have success.

## Garlic trivia and more

The Latin name for garlic is *Allium sativum*. A member of the lily family, it grows best in hot, dry climates. China, South Korea, India, and the U.S. are the top producers, and it is also grown in Egypt, France, Italy, and Spain. About 300 varieties are cultivated today, in shades of white, pink, red, and purple.

**APPENDIX III.**

Elephant garlic isn't really garlic after all, but actually a member of the leek family. It is milder and less flavorful than garlic, but makes up for it in sheer size. One head can weigh as much as a pound and can grow as big around as a grapefruit.

The rumor that garlic repels vampires probably began in the Middle Ages, when people hung garlic on doors to protect against witches.

Garlic is used in cooking almost all over the world. Stockholm and Finland have all-garlic restaurants, and the one in San Francisco is appropriately named The Stinking Rose.

Ancient Egyptians, who believed you could "take it with you," were buried with garlic in their tombs.

"Tomatoes and oregano make it Italian; wine and tarragon make it French. Sour cream makes it Russian; lemon and cinnamon make it Greek. Soy sauce makes it Chinese; garlic makes it good."

—ALICE MAY BROCK, ALICE'S RESTAURANT

"Without garlic I simply would not care to live."

—LOUIS DIAT, 1885–1957,
CHEF AT RITZ HOTELS AND INVENTOR OF VICHYSSOISE

"It is not really an exaggeration to say that peace and happiness begin, geographically, where garlic is used in cooking."

—X. MARCEL BOULESTIN, 1878–1943,
CHEF AND COOKBOOK AUTHOR